Go S

Written by Marcia Vaughan

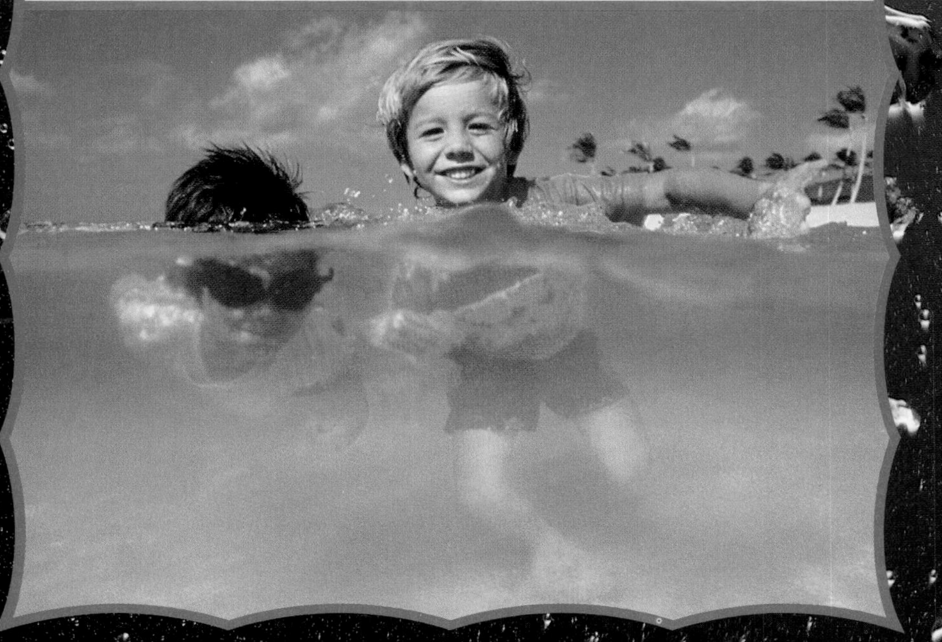

CELEBRATION PRESS
Pearson Learning Group

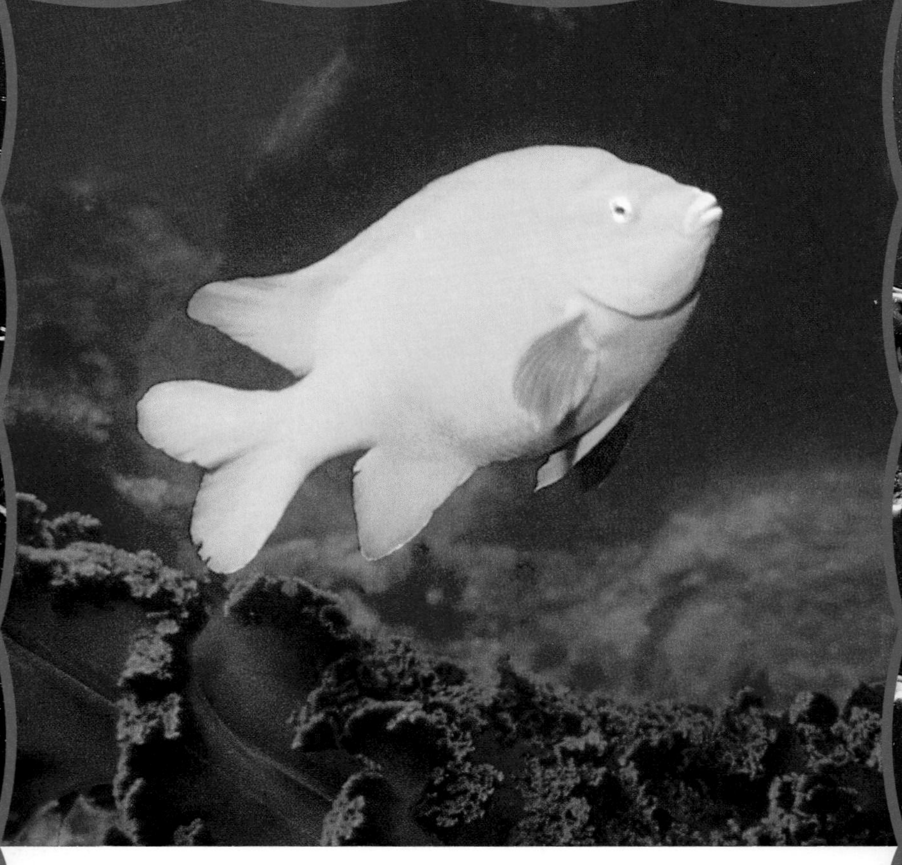

A fish,

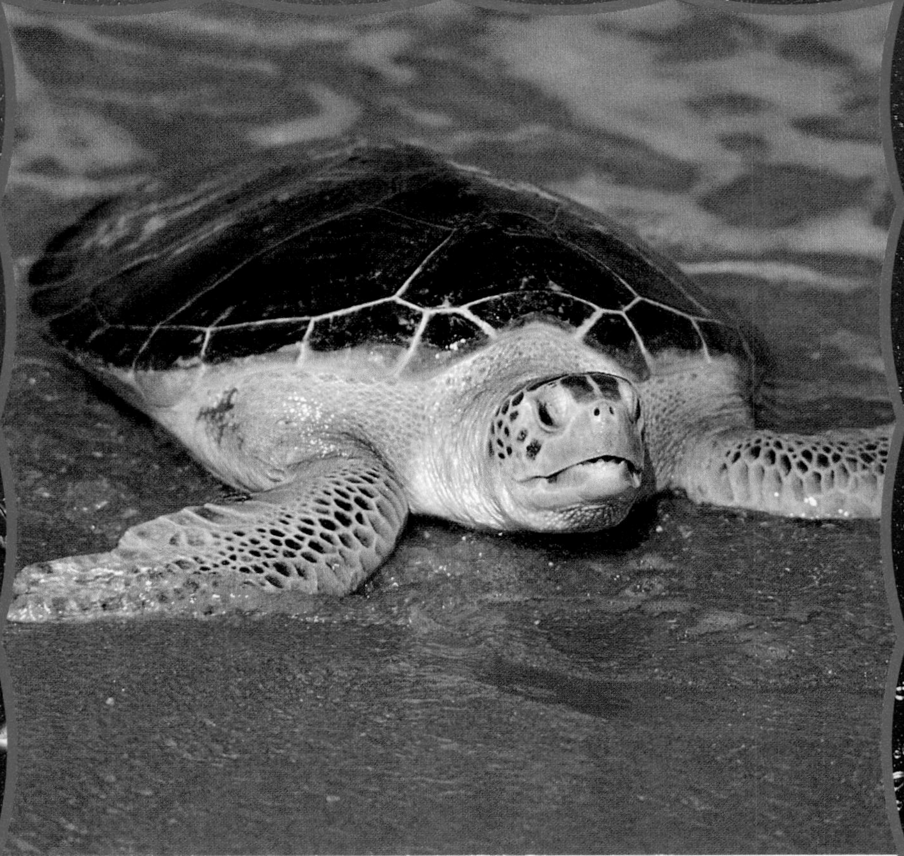

a turtle,

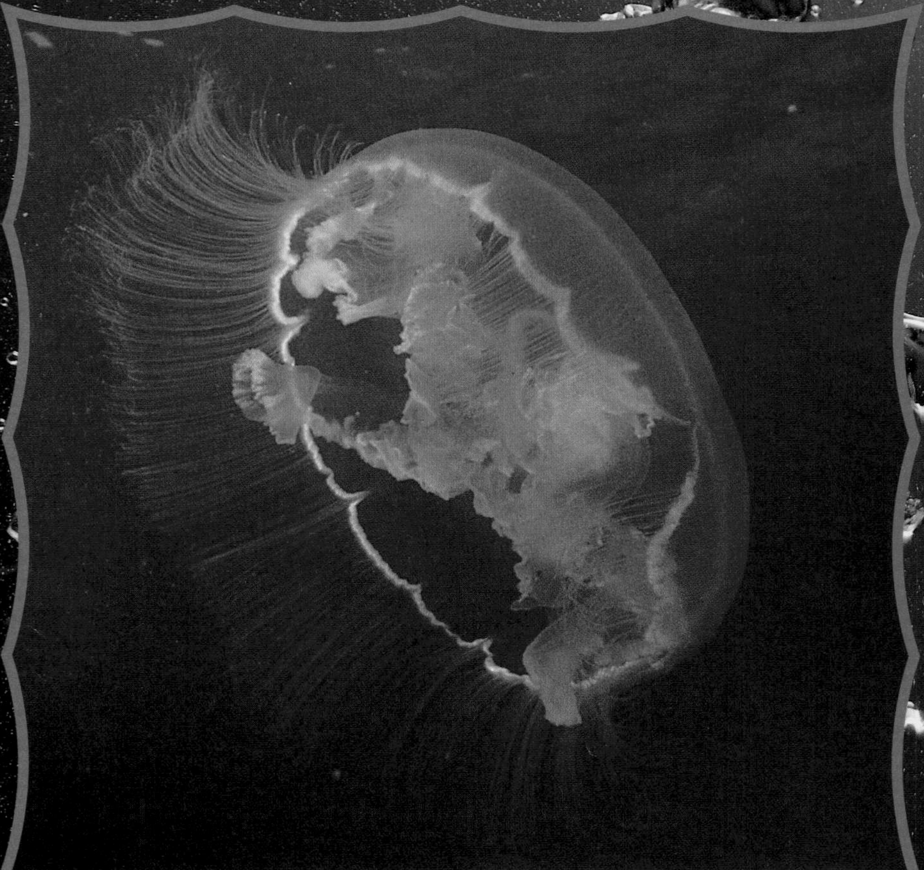

a jellyfish,

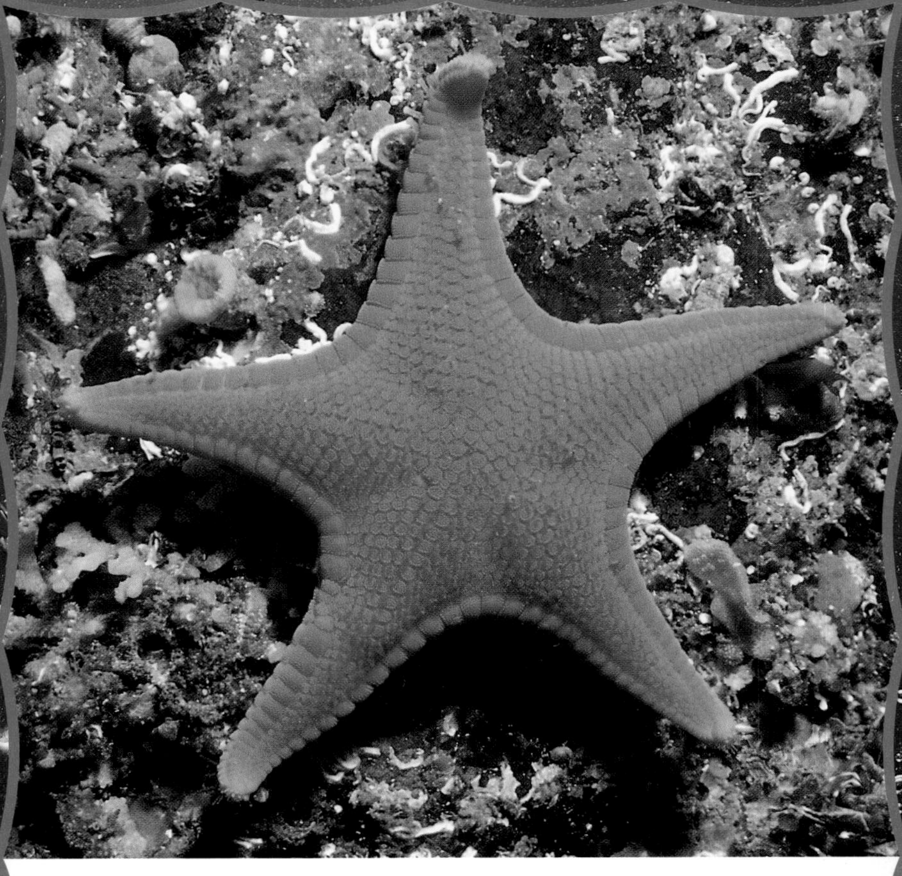

a sea star,

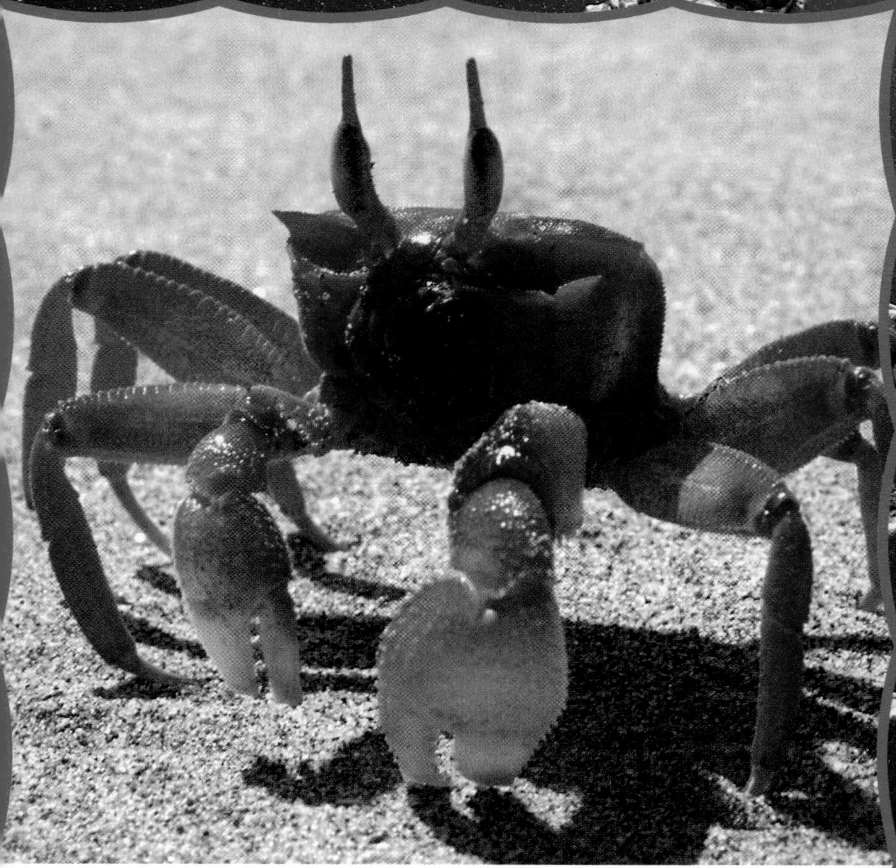

a crab,

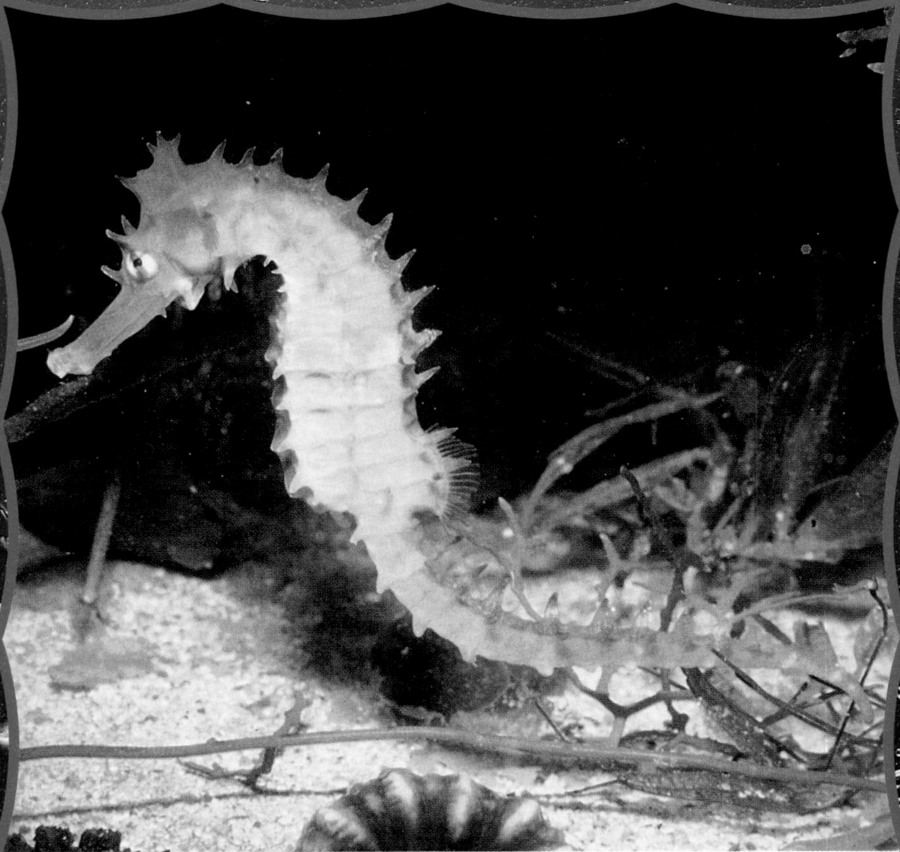

a sea horse . . .

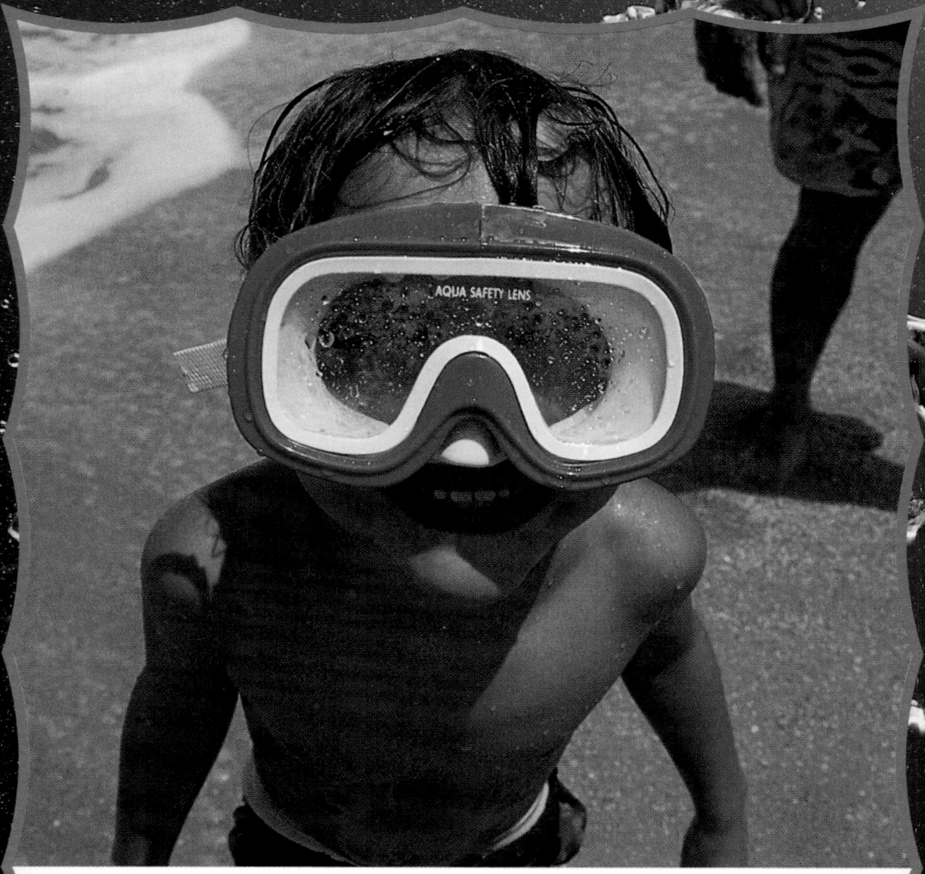

and me!